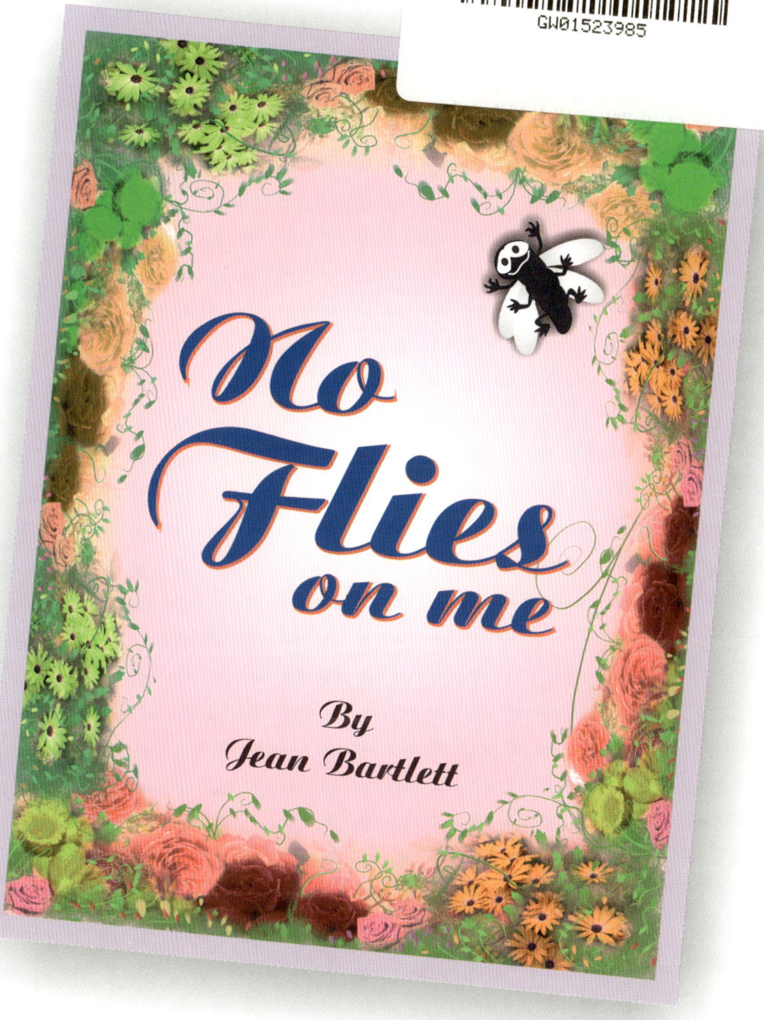
No
Flies
on me
By
Jean Bartlett

Jean Bartlett

*To Allan
and my family*

Contents

A Special Place	1
No Flies on Me	2
Walter	4
Our World	6
My Little Dog	8
Bicycle Ride	10
Bert	12
Nature's Beauty	13
Learning to Dance	14
A Gift of Flowers	16
Diet Time	18
Rosemary	20
The Harp	22
Feelings	23
I like my Coffee	24
A Nice Cup of Tea	26
Supermarket	28
Narrow Boat Trip	30
A Wonderful Place	32
Declaration	34
The Itch	36
Market Day	38
Lazy Sunday	40
Ageless	42
A life I Adore	44
The Intruder	46
A Day on a Bus	48
A Perfect Day	50
My Cat is a Queen	52
Lazy Day	54

A Special Place

There is a place, in my minds eye.
Will I find it? I breathe a sigh.
For I have been looking for many years,
With thoughts of gladness, sometimes, tears.

I have pondered so often, will I find this haven.
A lovely spot with wondrous views
A building of character, fine paths there laden
With bottle top windows, in a quaint small mews.

I can see myself there, drinking tea.
In an atmosphere relaxing to me.
I'd feel safe and secure
More than I have ever known
It could be a place, I could call home.

Somewhere to enjoy, and relax when I need.
Away from any noise, a place I can read.
It stands on a slope, an incline, a hill.
I look into my mind to know it would thrill.

To find a place of my dreams,
Where time stands still.
I will find it some day,
I know that I will.

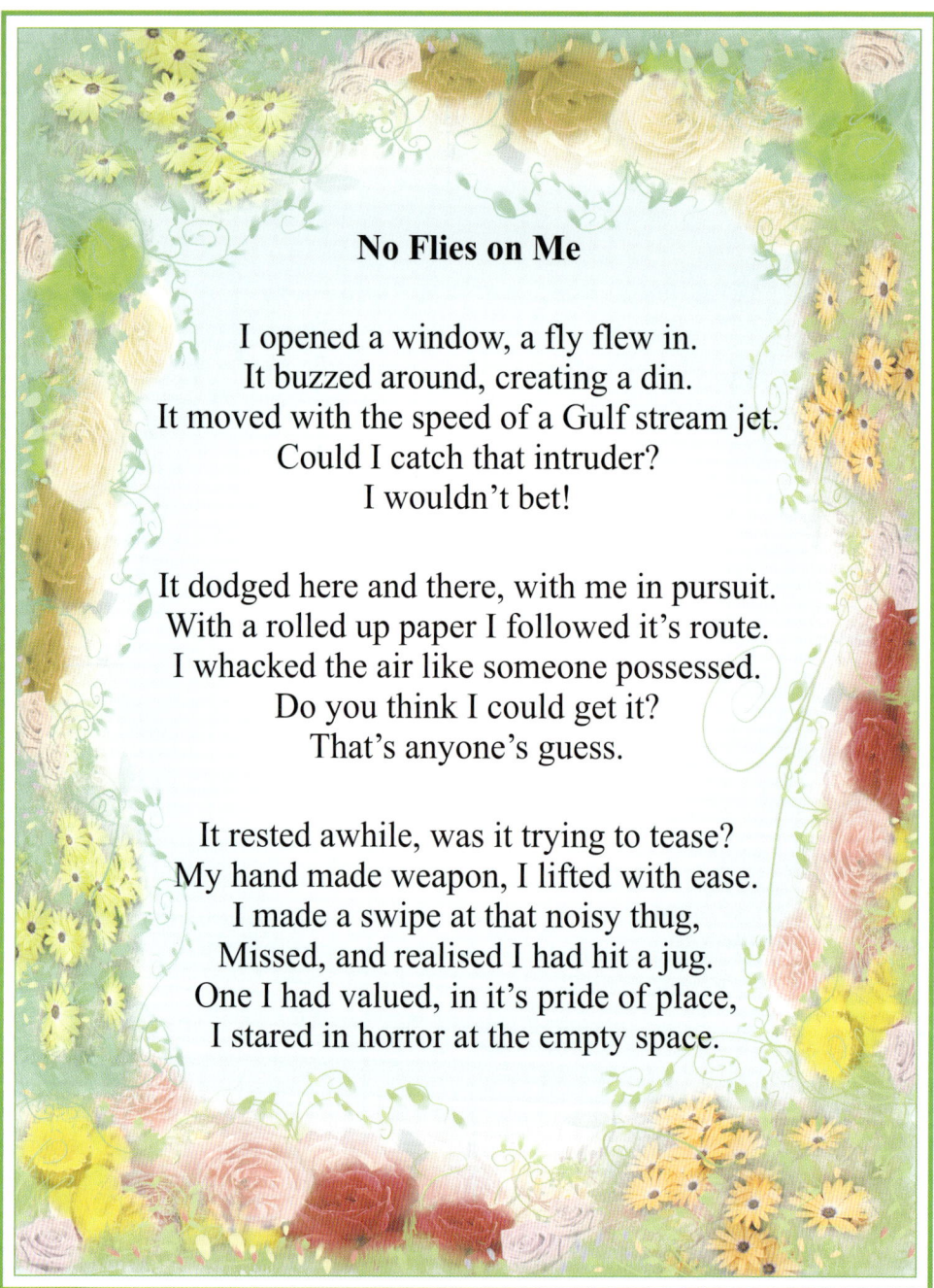

No Flies on Me

I opened a window, a fly flew in.
It buzzed around, creating a din.
It moved with the speed of a Gulf stream jet.
Could I catch that intruder?
I wouldn't bet!

It dodged here and there, with me in pursuit.
With a rolled up paper I followed it's route.
I whacked the air like someone possessed.
Do you think I could get it?
That's anyone's guess.

It rested awhile, was it trying to tease?
My hand made weapon, I lifted with ease.
I made a swipe at that noisy thug,
Missed, and realised I had hit a jug.
One I had valued, in it's pride of place,
I stared in horror at the empty space.

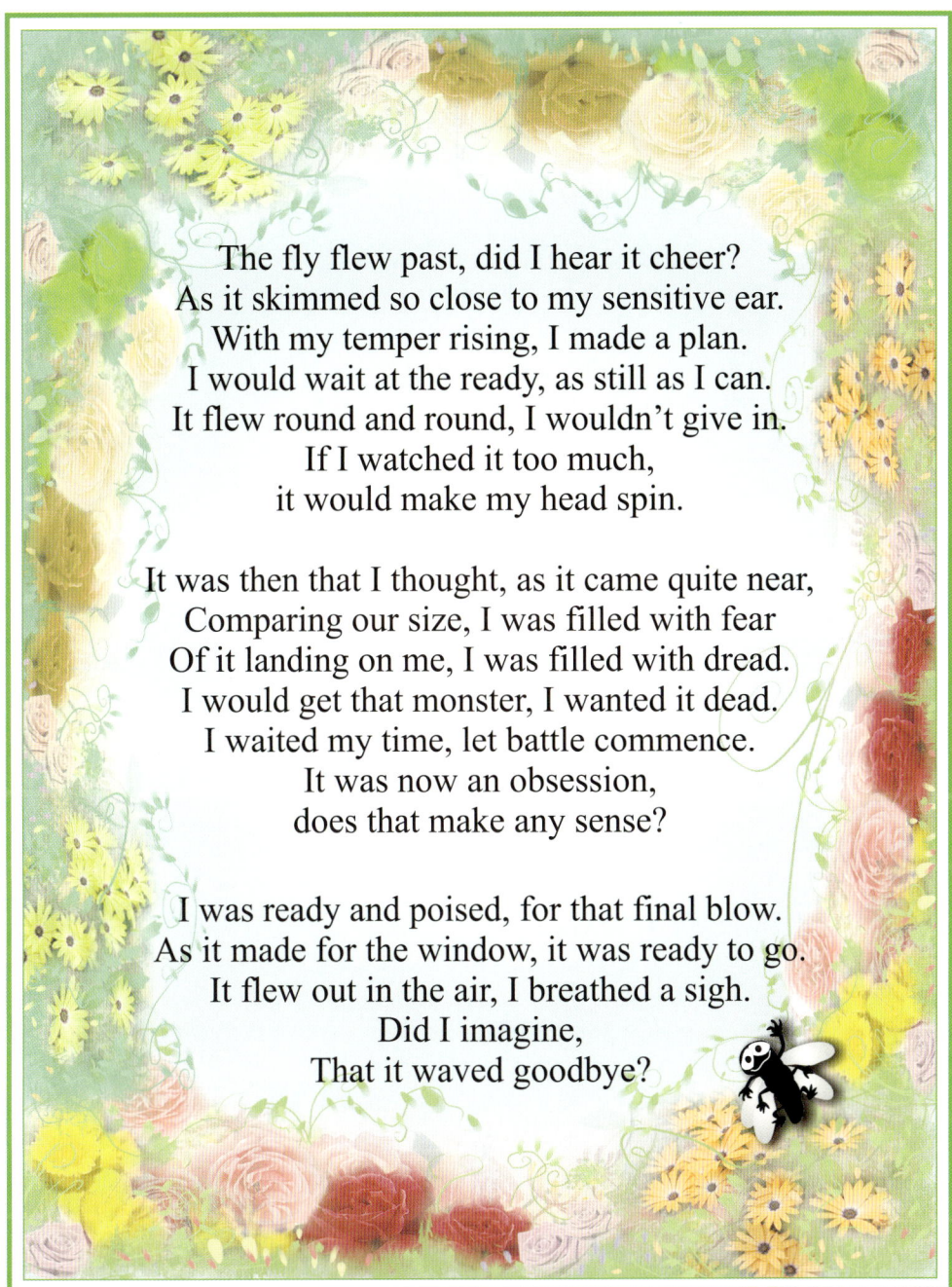

The fly flew past, did I hear it cheer?
As it skimmed so close to my sensitive ear.
With my temper rising, I made a plan.
I would wait at the ready, as still as I can.
It flew round and round, I wouldn't give in.
If I watched it too much,
it would make my head spin.

It was then that I thought, as it came quite near,
Comparing our size, I was filled with fear
Of it landing on me, I was filled with dread.
I would get that monster, I wanted it dead.
I waited my time, let battle commence.
It was now an obsession,
does that make any sense?

I was ready and poised, for that final blow.
As it made for the window, it was ready to go.
It flew out in the air, I breathed a sigh.
Did I imagine,
That it waved goodbye?

Walter

Walter is a pigeon
I call him Walt, for short.
I feed him bread most every day,
His head nods when he walks.
He is as nervous as a kitten,
He's cute and very shy.
When he looks up and sees me
He flies up to the sky.

His feathers are smooth,
His head is proud,
To get too close
Would not be allowed.
He is wild and free,
But between you and me
When he's just outside
He's good company for me.

Our World

What is happening to our world?
The facts relating are unfurled.
The hole is widening, environmental stress,
Icebergs melting, can our feelings we suppress?

Toxics flow into rivers and streams,
Chemicals, pollution, what does this mean?
Trees decreasing, land diminishing,
What are all these things accomplishing?

The sea will rise, more land we will lose,
Is it out of our hands, or can we choose?
To stop it now, in our defence.
To nip it in the bud is common sense.

Our treasured meadows and fields of green,
Wonderful scenery of a world serene.
Places flooding, temperatures rising,
Yes! We're worried, it's not surprising.

Did we predict it before, are we being naïve?
Do we choose to ignore it and disbelieve?
Did this happen in days gone by?
Or is it the future, are we left to cry?

To think of our children, grandchildren too.
Are we making a world, when this day we will rue?
Is it time to change, before it's too late?
When do we decide to seal our fate?

My Little Dog

When he looks at me with his soulful eyes.
That change so quickly, to complete surprise.
I often think that he can read my mind
Almost human, and one of a kind.

He runs to his basket to bring me his toy
One he has had that very day.
I tell him then, he is such a good boy.
If I try to take it from him,
He will run away.

The wealth of affection that he gives to me.
When he gives me his paw, and then sits on my knee.
Of a million to one selection, there could never be
Another one just like him.
Yes! He's the one for me.

I can't believe how smart he is, and am always so amazed
He seems to know the words I say, and
Answers to my phrase.
I know I couldn't part with him; he's loyal and loving too.
I was there right from the start with him,
I love him through and through.

His soft brown coat, his waggly tail
And cute expressions never fail,
To cheer me up, with his comical ways.
A wonderful therapy, to fill my days.

He never takes advantage of my kindness and my praise.
Even when he's on a rampage, it's just a little phase.
He couldn't be more loving, I could never ask for more,
He's my pal, my friend, my little dog.
The one that I adore.

A Bicycle Ride

I cycled along roads past fields of green
To many places I had never been.
Up hills and dales, troughs and valleys,
With speeds as fast as in a Rally.

I'd polished my cycle until it gleamed
When I looked at it, it made me beam
The frame was red, wheels were silver
I had to admit, it was a great mover.

The freshening winds, upon my face
My lungs filled with air, as I kept the pace.
I passed a stream, twisting and turning
I enjoyed it so much, my heart was yearning.

I stayed out all night and slept in the dark,
Continued on when I heard a lark.
I can go anywhere without a care,
I could travel the world, that's if I dare.

Whether alone or with a friend
From start to finish, I enjoy every bend.
The glorious scenery, the waterfalls
Past rippling streams, and across the moors.

I don't need to hike
For there's one thing I like,
Travelling around on
My dear bike.

Bert

Bert is a frog
He lives on a stone,
In a nice little pond
The place he calls home.

He sits there and croaks
And has a fine green coat.
He hops from place to place,
And keeps himself afloat.

He puffs out his neck
And catches small flies
He keeps very quiet
With his bulging eyes.

Children like to stroke him
He sits there like a lamb,
Suddenly, he jumps away
Saying, catch me if you can.

Nature's Beauty

I saw some flowers, upon a hill,
That had the power, my heart to thrill.
Yellow, green and purple hue,
As I approached, a clearer view.

Standing there with heads held high,
Basking in sunshine, I gave a sigh.
I sat for a while, midst this creation,
With peaceful thoughts and true sensation.

I wandered on, and over the hill,
There were buttercups, daisies and marigolds too,
Across the meadows, beyond the trees,
A colourful sight my thoughts to seize.
Among many foxgloves, growing wildly,
Lilacs and pinks, with centres of ivory.

I wanted to paint them,
My heart was yearning,
Just like a flame within me burning.
I stretched my legs
And quickened my step
Canvas and paints, back home to get.

If I could capture this nature's beauty,
I felt it my yearning,
I felt it my duty.
Display it somewhere for all to see,
To give them pleasure,
As it gave me.

Learning to Dance

Do I start with my right foot, or was it my left,
I'm ready and raring to go.
I wait for the music, in anticipation
Lose my balance and stub my big toe.
My co-ordination is failing me badly,
My rhythm is painfully slow,
My stance is so different
And style non-existent
I confess to be miserably low.

I step to the left, it should be the right
I'm standing on toes, as if I'm in flight.
My arms should be up, but hanging right down
The instructor is smiling, or was that a frown?
They said I'll get better, maybe next week
The way that I'm going it looks very bleak

I waltz and I chassis, I'm taking a chance
I'm doing my best, my steps to enhance.
I move a bit quicker, my confidence grows.
Why is everyone looking at my graceful pose?
I've suddenly realised, whilst they're watching me prance
They're laughing their socks off,
For it's the wrong dance.

I'm learning the Tango, and then the Fandango,
My morale is feeling quite drastic.
They taught me to turn,
Some points I could learn
You would think I was made of elastic,
As I felt myself spinning around and around,
I felt my cheeks burning as I slipped to the ground.

A Gift of Flowers

I cannot imagine anything more,
When a gift of flowers
Arrive at my door.
The excitement I feel,
And pleasure within,
A perfect way for the day to begin.
A bouquet of flowers, a bunch, a rose,
Can lift my heart, from a moments repose.
As I busy myself with daily chores,
I pass by my flowers,
And have to pause,
To admire the colours, the leaves and display,
A second's glance can make my day.
It is hard to envisage the way I feel,
If my vase is empty, with lonely appeal.
I need flowers in life,
The feelings I treasure,
A constant look of pride and pleasure.
If in my time, with my share of flowers,
I can think of the happiness, and many hours,
They have given me, to my hearts content,
I will remember with love,
Who gave or sent,
A gift of flowers.

Diet Time

I'm starting a diet, the day after tomorrow.
To-day, I made up my mind
The thought of this just fills me with sorrow,
To leave all the goodies behind.

I still have two days in which to indulge
I can eat anything I see.
The amount that I have I can't really divulge,
A secret known only to me.

I will weigh myself before I begin,
I'll strip my clothes right off.
I imagine a voice from deep within,
Saying, will one of you please get off?

I'll stand on the scales,
Trust the weight to be fair.
I'm sure it cheated last time.
I admit I had one leg in the air,
For I thought that the scales were unkind.

I would run up and down the stairs if I could,
Not too quick, but then not too slow.
It could be a problem, now I think again.
For I live in a bungalow.

I'll give up the chocolates, cakes and the biscuits
Including fats and cheese.
I'll stick out my chin, I'm going to risk it
For I would love to see
Both my knees.

Then when I am slim, I'll go to the gym.
And run fifteen miles a day.
I'll be slim round the hips
Shall I have Fish and chips?
Hey! I'm not on a diet today.

Rosemary

She looks at me with unseeing eyes,
She seems almost real with a look that is wise.
Her blond curly hair and blue grey eyes
She has a captivating look, almost of surprise.

She wears a dress, with grey stripes and red
She doesn't change when its time for bed.
There are red velvet cuffs and the neck has a bow,
White lace is threaded, through a hem that is low

A red velvet hat and pretty white shoes,
Handle them carefully or one you may lose.
She sits on a sideboard, as if looking around,
She never cries, not even a sound.

She is pretty and sweet and always looks neat
A friend when I need her, my secrets to keep.
Although she can't answer, I love her dearly
When I talk to her sometime's it makes me see clearly.

Inspire's courage and peace,
when her eyes I meet
A confidante and true pal,
Rosemary, my china doll.

The Harp

I thought the Harp I'd learn to play,
Then strum a tune most every day.
I bought a nice one, very tall,
Got it through the door, but it stuck in the hall.

I pulled it and pushed it, but still it was wedged.
I had to climb over it to go to bed.
I lifted my foot, and lost my balance,
Had to hang on to the hall curtain valance.

It was leaning to one side, my face was red.
I tried to push it, but it fell on my head.
Next day I managed, to get it in the room.
I was so angry, I nearly hit it with a broom.

Then I sat down, put my hands on the strings.
I'd hardly started to twang it, when I heard it go ping.
I got out the music, though the strings were less
I tried to play a tune, but it really was a mess.

I looked at the music it made me frown,
I couldn't believe my foolishness, for I had it upside down.
I don't know why I started it, was it really for a lark,
I think I'll give it serious thought, before I learn to play the harp.

Feelings

Happy feelings to awake at dawn,
Banish sadness, or feelings forlorn
Shout from the roof top, feelings of love,
Thankful for sunshine in skies above

Feelings of friendship from one to another
A gift of life, of a baby to mother.
An abundance of love between two people,
Knowing each other's thoughts and feelings.

Thinking as one, the power of telepathy
Projecting as one in perfect empathy.
Feelings of parting, time after time
In all walks of life of many kinds.

Being together at the end of the day,
Laughter of children out at play.
A myriad of feelings for life to begin
An integral part of happiness within.

I Like my Coffee

I stretched my arms and then my legs,
Poked my toe right out of bed.
For the aroma of coffee, I lifted my nose
Slowly percolating on the stove.

Then I heard a stealthy tread,
Coming up the stairs and to my bed
He had the cup upon the tray,
Intoxicating beans were attacking my brain.

When it arrived, I stirred in the cream,
Put my cup to my lips, the taste was a dream.
Then I was awake and feeling fit,
I started to get ready for the Sunday trip.

When I was dressed and ready to go,
A further cup gave me a glow.
As sip by sip, it slithered down
I liked it so much, in it I could drown.

We sat by the river in pensive mood,
With a nice cup of coffee, and plenty of food.
Then lazed away the afternoon.
We drank some more coffee, it was over too soon.

Later that day we strolled through the fields,
Enjoying our thoughts, and what they can yield.
I thought of home, and the percolator,
The coffee smell, and it's creator.

There are so many things that we can enjoy,
Of basic things and Hoi Polloi.
A tasty cake or a treacle toffee.
But most of all, I like my coffee.

A Nice Cup of Tea.

Every teapot has its story.
Strong or weak, hot or cold.
The drink within, in all it's glory,
Tells a tale, since days of old.

Its welcome taste, never ending.
In every walk of life there is.
A consequential flavour descending,
To a favourite vessel, it can give.

In every mood and situation.
To all requirements, want or need
A truly welcome, warm sensation.
For every culture, class, or creed.

Many varieties, numerous tastes
Drink it slowly, or in haste.
Nice with a biscuit on a plate.
Never too early, never too late.

Whenever you need it. So easy to make.
A popular drink, for your buds to take.
If you're feeling low, it's easy to see
All you need then, is a nice cup of tea.

The Supermarket

I collect the trolley at the door,
Supermarket, there's food galore
Up one aisle, and down another
They've moved things again, I discover.

On and on, the tannoys blazing
The number of times, now that is amazing.
The children are noisy, be quiet! I insist
Then I realize I've forgotten my list.

I don't need very much, and then I see,
Oh! That may come in useful,
Its buy one, get one free.
Gloomy assistants stock the shelves
Blocking the aisles, from hands to delve.

The children are running,
Don't touch that please Jack.
I stare in horror, at the crumbling stack.
As I rush to the tills, Oh! What a hash.
I hand over my card, they smile, any cash?

A pleasant assistant helps me to pack,
I've forgotten something, I'm not going back.
When I came in the weather was fine,
Now it's raining is that a sign?

With all the hastle,
The privilege is mine,
I shall have it delivered
Then order on line.

The Narrow Boat Trip

Cruising along in a narrow boat,
It gave to me a life of hope.
Relaxing in a pensive mood,
With a drink in my hand and plenty of food

I saw many ducks and ducklings too
A host of animals for us to view.
The banks, the flowers and trees of green
A casual life, as in a dream.

The sun was shining the day was kind,
We saw grey swans, and in good time,
They would turn to white then we would find
Hold their heads high and look refined.

The Kingfisher with its feathers so blue
Flew low over the water, close to me too.
As it passed by, I thought of the sky
On a beautiful day with its colourful hue.

I saw a Marina with many boats,
"Bliss" "Freewheeler" and "In my own time"
There was also one called "Jersey Lillie"
The colour was bright and curtains frilly.

Birds were singing, it was easy to see
Why this wealth of nature gave pleasure to me.
Cruising along contentedly,
So much to learn, and lots to see.

Bridges and fishing, folks having tea,
Wonderful scenery, my heart filled with glee.
A step from the rat race, precious moments of time,
The only thing lacking, I wish it were mine.

A wonderful place.

I open my eyes, what do I see?
Fields of green, a branch of a tree.
Rolling fields, skies of blue.
A host of flowers in colourful hue.

I sit here amazed at nature's creation.
Scenery around, fills me with elation.
Our beautiful land for all to see.
A wonderful place on earth to be.

I often wonder of many things.
A creature's life, a bird on a wing.
The mere existance of life itself.
The value of this abundance of wealth.

I close my eyes, then remember the scene.
Of the many places that I have been.
I feel quite humble, so very glad,
To appreciate, the gift of life we have.

Declaration

He held her hand along the way,
Not a word was spoken, they could not say,
About the love, they knew they shared
Of thoughts of love, and how they cared.

They strolled along through fields of green,
With wonderful thoughts, they could not seem
To express their love, they had for each other.
To say the words, from one to another.

Suddenly, he then declared
My life, my heart, I have to share.
I need to spend each day with you,
Without your love, what will I do?

She immediately knew how,
To seal the moment here and now.
I can tell you that my love is true,
My life I always want with you.

As they continued on there way,
They knew that on this very day
Their love declared was strong and true,
Would last them both, their whole life through.

The Itch

I had an itch the other day,
In the middle of my back.
To find out how to scratch it,
My brains I had to rack.
I tried to stretch my arm around,
I almost reached the spot.
It seemed a massive area,
For such a little dot.

I struggled then, it drove me mad,
My foot I had to stamp.
The position that I held my arm,
Was giving me the cramp.
I thought and thought, what can I do?
The itch was getting stronger.
I had to find a solution;
I couldn't stand it any longer.

I thought about a pencil,
A long stick or a rule.
It crossed my mind oh! Just my luck,
It really was quite cruel…
Why wasn't it on my finger?
Or my ankle or my knee?
I wish that I could reach it;
From the itch, I would be free…

I had an idea, right there and then,
My thoughts began to soar,
Once and for all, I'll be rid of this,
I walked up to the door.
This intruder had its notice,
The offender I did tame,
I turned around and rubbed my back,
Hard against the frame.

The relief it gave came flooding through;
It reached right through my veins,
It seemed to be all over the place,
Like following a chicane.
I know you can imagine it,
For you've been through it too,
The next time when you have an itch,
You'll know just what to do…

Market Day

The market, the market is here today,
With lots of lovely food, hooray,
There's apple pies and rhubarb too,
And lots of others filled with fruit.

There are cheeses like you've never seen,
Homegrown cabbage, caulis and beans.
Wines galore, you can have a taste.
Don't spill a drop, that would be a waste.

The coffee smells, they drive you crazy,
To sit all day and drink till you're hazy.
There are duck eggs and hen eggs
Big ones too, some for me and some for you.

There are meats galore in prices varying,
It's not the place if you're vegetarian.
Bacon and sausage, you cannot resist,
If you carry too much you can strain your wrist.

You're tempted to buy, and then you sigh,
To spend so much money as you walk by.
You've bought lots of food, and paid the bill,
Emptied your purse and you feel quite ill.

Then off you go, you've walked 'till you've dropped,
And filled the fridge right up to the top.
You say you'll economise, but find,
You will spend just as much
When you go next time.

Lazy Sunday

I'm having a lazy Sunday,
I may even sleep over til' Monday.
I'll have breakfast in bed, some toast and an egg
I may even make it a fun day.

I could go for a walk, or just sit and talk
Drink coffee all day, have my own way.
I may do my keep fit, wiggle toes where I sit.
Soak my feet for a bit, or perhaps sit and knit.

I'm having a lazy Sunday
Out of seven, it's only the one day.
Won't rise with the lark, may sleep until dark.
Do nothing all day, or go to the park.

I could go to the seaside, paddle my feet.
Lie in a deck chair, for a special treat.
I could go for a swim, then to the gym.
It sounds like hard work, I think I'll stay in.

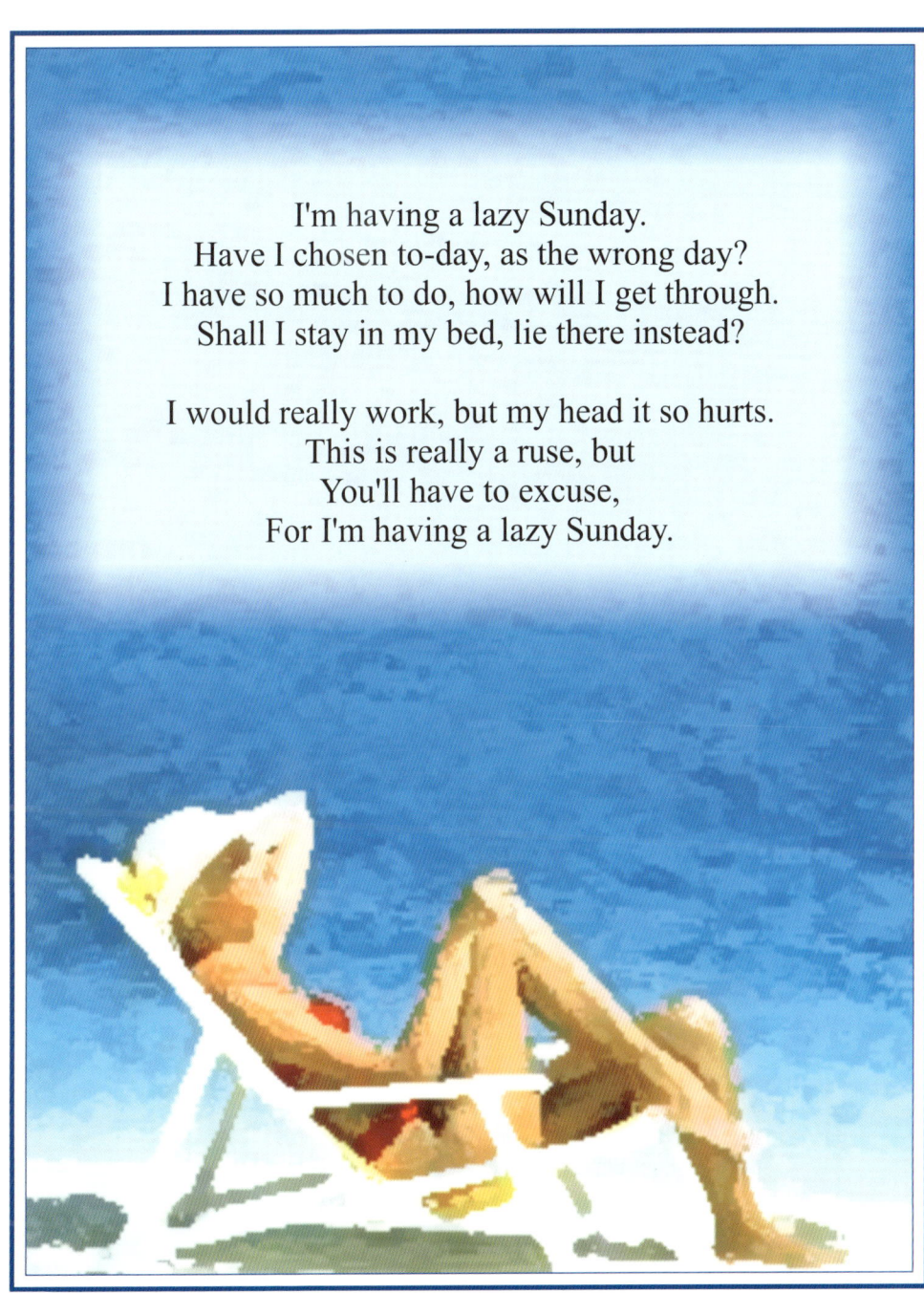

I'm having a lazy Sunday.
Have I chosen to-day, as the wrong day?
I have so much to do, how will I get through.
Shall I stay in my bed, lie there instead?

I would really work, but my head it so hurts.
This is really a ruse, but
You'll have to excuse,
For I'm having a lazy Sunday.

Ageless

They say that age is a number,
I'd rather the digits be less
When I looked in the mirror this morning,
The image gave nothing but stress.

The figure I saw standing before me
With it's double chin, wrinkles and all,
Reminded me of a great Hippo
Bulging eyes, a big nose, but not tall.

My bones like the tin man in Wizard
Creak noisily, each time I walk.
And my hair like the straw man on his way to Oz
Is straggly, like his made of straw.

My waist is quite slender I imagine,
I tried a belt to see whether it fits.
But when I stood looking at the reflection before me,
You can't see the belt for my hips.

I'm not really ugly, not very,
But then I'm not looking for passes
I think I'm quite nice, if you look at me twice
Or I look at myself with my glasses.

Sometimes when I go out walking.
I try to walk like a model I find.
Don't worry! I have no illusions
For I'd hate to be walking behind.

At the end of the day, I am me, I can say
For spirit, I really have plenty.
Don't mimic my stance, I could lead you a dance
My cup is quite full, never empty.

A Life I Adore.

I woke up early, the Maid walked in.
She placed a tray right under my chin.
The aroma of coffee, a satisfying smell.
A healthy breakfast to keep me well.
She walked to the window to draw the curtains,
Then she ran my bath, of that I'd be certain.

Then I got dressed in my Sunday best
And waited for James, my personal driver.
To bring round the Limo, the colour was cream
For quality and comfort, it was a dream.

I went for a drive and visited friends,
In luxury style, along roads and round bends.
Then I had my lunch at a classy Hotel.
And afterwards coffee, a wonderful smell.

Then I stepped back into my car.
I am rich and famous, for I am a star.
I arrived back home, from my leisurely day
And was met by the cook, with her little book.
I gave her instructions for an evening dinner,
But whatever she did, it was always a winner.

Later on, I dressed for the evening.
A wealth of splendour was given to all.
Then at the end, when the guests were leaving
Someone nudged me, and started to call.
"Come on" said a voice, "Where is my coffee"?
I opened my eyes, it then revealed all.

That I had been dreaming, it came as a shock.
I lifted my head and looked at the clock.
Did I dream of a life that I wanted instead?
I looked at my husband, and got out of bed.
Gave him a peck, and to myself said
What could I want more?
It's never a bore,
For I have a family, and a life I adore.

The Intruder

As I lay sleeping through the night.
A sudden noise gave me a fright.
I lay quite still, hardly daring to breathe,
My nose was itching I wanted to sneeze.

I heard it again, that disturbing noise.
Should I put the light on, or was that wise?
Then I realised it came from below
I got out of bed, and stubbed my toe.

As scared as I was, I cursed the bedpost.
Put on the light, then checked the coast.
I stealthily crept towards the stairs,
Was this a dream,full of nightmares?

I realised then I was fully awake,
Put my shoulders back, for steps to take.
Grabbed the end of the vacuum
For a means of protection,
Listened for the noise from which direction.

I heard it again, and jumped three feet.
Was that a rattle? No! it was my teeth.
I bravely descended for I realised then,
It was outside the door, there it was again.

No one was inside, I checked with dread.
I was shaking so much, should have stayed in bed.
It was a weird kind of noise, had I heard it before?
A gentle pat on the knocker of my door.
I carefully opened, then I said, "Oh drat"
It wasn't an intruder; it was next door's cat.

A Day on a Bus

We had an idea the other day,
We would get on a bus and ride all the way.
We stayed on the bus until the furthest stop,
Enjoyed it much more, for we sat at the top.

We watched many people getting on getting off,
Were they going to work? Or about to shop?
As the day went by, I found it quite soothing.
The thought of doing this, we found quite amusing.
Could have driven there and back in half the time,
The idea being was to relax my mind.

Get away from the wheel of the constant driving.
See the things, I normally don't see.
An abundance of flowers, a study of faces
A blade of grass, or a leaf of a tree.

Browsing and glancing, as passengers do.
Seeing shop windows come into view.
We passed through the countryside, and
As we looked around, saw an
Abundance of nature, with scenery abound.

As we sat there, through the window I gazed,
My memories stirring of childhood days.
When we used to play without any cares,
We were seldom bored, that was very rare.

When we reached the last stop,
The stairs we descended.
We wandered around for a while.
It wasn't a place that we had intended,
But pleasant with plenty of style.

We found a good tearoom recommended to me.
The food was exquisite and tasty.
Apple pie with ice cream, an abundance of fruit,
With wonderful, melt in the mouth pastry.

After walking around, enjoying the views,
Made our way back for our trip to return.
Our memories of this, we would not want to lose,
For our friends, a suggestion it earned.

We arrived back home, reflecting the day,
So much fun since
We couldn't think when.
Our day on the bus, was so good for us,
In the future we would do it again.

A Perfect Day

Daisies, buttercups, many wild flowers,
I strolled among for many hours.
Grassy plains, rolling hills
Alone with my thoughts, my head to fill.
This tranquil scene, as life intended
To soak the earth with my very being.

I passed through trees, standing proud.
The after rain and clearing cloud.
A glistening drop, upon a leaf
Falls like a tear, to the ground beneath.

I came upon a rippling stream,
Clear and shallow I could see
A multitude of shiny stones,
Numerous shades, of many tones.
Movement of water, creating sun-catchers
A glorious view in their restful home.

As I stood there, in pensive thought,
I welcomed the calm, in which I sought,
Escape in my soul from racing time.
To a world of peace, quiet, sublime.

I found a place, and there I sat,
Deep in thought, I imagined that
I could paint a picture, of this wonderful scene.
With lightness of heart, where I could dream.

I would keep this time within my heart
To treasure there, an integral part
Of the day when I enhanced my life
With the beauty there, released from strife.
Another time to feel new thoughts
Within the lap of nature's course.

My Cat Is a Queen

A shower of silk describes her fur.
A gleaming form, beyond compare
Reclining there in restful pose,
She stretches her legs, and then her toes.

As she looks at me, with her knowing stare
The feelings of love inside we share
She often purrs when I stroke her back,
Her comical capers, she never lacks.
A ball of wool, a piece of string
Amuses more than anything.

When I leave her for a while
I sometimes have a confident smile,
Knowing when I return again
She will be waiting,
My furry friend.

Greeting me with her friendly tone,
Telling me, she is glad I'm home.
After food and drink
She settles near me,
Showing contentment in every way
When nodding off her eyes are bleary
*A wonderful queen in every way.

An adult female cat is called a queen.

Lazy Day

Lazy day near rivers and streams,
Watching boats, I laze and dream
Lazy day away from crowds
Walking in meadows, under silver clouds.

Lazy day in fields of green
The sun shining bright to set the scene
Lazy day Reading a book
Or stare into space, a vacant look

Lazy day in fields of corn
Thinking of good times
Being glad, you were born
Lazy day your feelings to lend
A perfect day, from beginning to end.

© Jean Bartlett 2006
All rights reserved

Illustrations by Benjamin Sowa

Printed By Restart Print 01827 287196

Issue one